HERITAGE

The CELTS *in Britain*

Robert Hull

WAYLAND

Heritage

The Anglo-Saxons
The Celts in Britain
The Romans in Britain
The Tudors
The Victorians
The Vikings in Britain

Cover pictures: A bronze and enamel harness decoration, made in Britain around 100 BC (main picture). Part of a decoration on a bucket and gold coins of about AD 50, found in Kent (left). An enamelled bronze brooch made in Britain about AD 50 (right).

Editor: Rosemary Ashley
Designer: Jean Wheeler

First published in 1997 by
Wayland (Publishers) Limited,
61 Western Road, Hove,
East Sussex, BN3 1JD, England

British Library Cataloguing in Publication Data

Hull, Robert
  The Celts in Britain. - (Heritage)
  1. Civilization, Celtic - Juvenile literature 2. Celts - Great Britain - History - Juvenile literature 3. Celts - Great Britain - Social life and customs - To 1066 - Juvenile literature
  I. Title
  941'.01'089916

  ISBN 0750218223

Typeset by Jean Wheeler

Printed and bound by G. Canale & C.S.p.A., Turin, Italy

Contents

1 Who were the Celts?   4

2 When did the Celts settle in Britain and Ireland?   6

3 What crafts and skills did the Celts have?   10

4 What did the Celts look like?   14

5 How was Celtic life organized?   16

6 What religion and beliefs did the Celts have?   20

7 What stories did the Celts tell and what languages
did they speak?   24

8 What happened to the Celts?   28

Glossary   30

Books to Read   31

Places to Visit   31

Index   32

chapter one

WHO WERE
THE CELTS?

▶ *A Celtic horned helmet found in the River Thames, in London. It dates from about the first century AD.*

▼ *A decorated iron sword and scabbard made by a Celtic smith. Sometimes these were placed in the graves of rich chieftains, or left in sacred places as offerings to gods, perhaps after victory in battle.*

The Celts were one of the first great peoples of Europe. They helped to create the nations of Europe, and Britain and Ireland. At their strongest, round about 300 BC, their lands stretched from west of Ireland to Turkey, and from the Baltic Sea to the Mediterranean.

Although the Celts did not use writing for everyday purposes, we have clues about them, from objects which they left behind. Hidden coins, weapons thrown into rivers, dropped brooches, chariot wheels buried with dead chiefs. All these objects tell us something about the Celts.

But they left other evidence behind them: forts, walls, fields, villages. When we add all the clues on to what writers tell us about them, then we begin to piece together a picture about the Celts who came to Britain.

Britain and Ireland

The Celts left their homelands in Central Europe and began arriving in the islands of Britain (England, Scotland, Wales) and Ireland possibly as early as 700 BC. They came trading, or fleeing from war, or just settling with others. They built forts, houses, farms and villages. The remains of one small village can be seen at Chysauster in Cornwall.

Then the Roman invaders came, and after them the Anglo-Saxons, and thousands of Celts fled west, into Wales and Cornwall.

Not all Celts were threatened by invaders. Parts of Britain and Ireland have been Celtic for more than two thousand years. On islands off the coasts of Scotland and Ireland there are people to whom English is still a foreign language.

There are many traces of the first Celts in Britain and Ireland. There are Celtic forts; weapons, jewellery, tools, harnesses, chariot parts, winejars and bones fill thousands of museum cabinets. Celtic chiefs were sometimes buried with their chariots, as we can see from chariot-wheels found in burial chambers such as the one at Wetwang Slack in Yorkshire.

The first Celts lived near the source of the River Danube, in what is now Austria, between 700 and 400 BC. Soon after 400 BC huge numbers were on the move. They settled in Italy but the Romans drove them back over the Alps into northern Europe. In 52 BC the Roman general Julius Caesar defeated a great army of Celts, or Gauls, as he called them, and they came under Roman Rule.

▼ *The Celts have left hill forts all across Britain. This is Maiden Castle in Dorset, showing the ditch and a huge earth wall.*

chapter two

WHEN DID THE CELTS SETTLE IN
BRITAIN AND IRELAND?

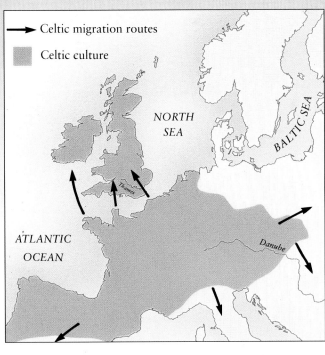

A map showing the routes of Celtic migrations in northern Europe.

Most Celts probably came to Ireland and Britain after 600 BC. They might have come in separate waves, or continuously trickled in as there had been trading and travel between Europe and Britain for hundreds of years. Most Celts probably came to join other Celts already living here.

▼ *This is the Isle of Barra, in the Hebrides. Here the ancient Celtic language is still very much alive – it is taught in schools and spoken in homes.*

◀ *An aerial photograph of the stone fort of Dun Conor, with its surrounding outbuildings and fields. It stands, half-ruined, on one of the Aran islands, off the south-west coast of Ireland.*

Forts and castles

In Britain and Ireland, as in Europe, the Celts settled in 'tribes'. Though these tribes were all Celt, with similar languages and ways of life, they often quarrelled amongst themselves. After they arrived, many tribes built forts of earth and wood, or stone.

In southern and western Britain and in Ireland the Celts built hill forts. In northern Scotland they built many small stone forts called 'duns' and circular towers of stone called 'brochs'. In all parts of Britain and Ireland they also built farms and hamlets, and there were probably some large settlements that were not strongly defended.

A traveller in the fifth century BC called Ireland and Britain the 'Pretanic' islands. The Celtic word 'Prydain' is modern Welsh for Britain. The Roman words 'Britannia' and 'Britanni' may be mispronunciations of a Celtic word.

In the sixth century BC, a traveller from the Greek colony of Massilia (Marseille) sailed round to the west coast of Spain. He learned that traders visited islands in the north called Ierne and Albion. Ierne comes from the same Celtic word as Eire, the name of the Irish state, and Albu was the old Irish name for Britain.

▶ *The hill fort of Danebury, showing part of the earth wall behind the winding entrance.*

Some historians think the Celts went to Ireland before they settled in Britain. They think this because, over the centuries, the Celts brought two different versions of the Celtic language. The earlier language has some 'q' or 'k' sounds where the other language has 'p'. For instance, the Gaelic spoken in Ireland and Scotland has 'mac' for 'son of'; in Welsh it is 'map'. Gaelic has 'ben' for mountain or summit, Welsh has 'pen'.

Danebury, near Winchester, in Hampshire, is the site of a Celtic hill fort that has been excavated by archaeologists. What they have found gives a vivid picture of the lives of some Celtic settlers in Britain after 500 BC. Just from walking around this hill fort you can see that the Celts who lived there expected trouble. Danebury was strongly fortified, and cleverly designed. At the top of the outer rampart was a steep wall of oak timbers with a bank of earth behind it for support. In front of the wall was a ditch. The entrance was twisty and complicated, with two sets of heavy gates.

Life in and around the fort

Danebury was ready for attack, but it was a place where people came on peaceful business, and where they lived and worked. Roads led into it. There were houses and farm buildings inside the walls. There were smithies for making weapons and tools, and ovens for breadmaking. There were granaries, with frames for drying corn. Some small square buildings were probably shrines for the gods. Fields surrounded the fort, filled with crops and grazing animals.

The Celts who lived in all these forts, castles, duns and brochs between 550 and 100 BC were probably chiefs and their families, and their warriors. The fort was a home for the rich and powerful. For others, it was a refuge in dangerous times.

Most people lived outside the fort, on lonely farms, or in circular houses grouped together in small hamlets. Often these hamlets produced all that the people needed. They made their own tools, threshed their own corn and baked bread in their ovens. Clothing was made in the home too, on upright looms.

The Celts were farmers. In many parts of Britain and Ireland the outlines of their fields are clear to see. Celtic fields are square or rectangular and are quite small, as they often still are in parts of Cornwall, Devon and western Ireland.

▼ *The stone entrance to Rochaill fort, Innishore, Aran. There would have been heavy wooden gates across the gap.*

chapter three

WHAT CRACRAFTS AND SKILLS DID THE CELTS HAVE?

Some of the Celts' greatest skills revolved around two things: their love of horses (the Irish still have this love) and their passion for decorating the objects they made and used.

The Celts were skilled miners, and brilliant metalworkers. They worked in bronze and later in iron. They made all kinds of strong weapons and tools. The speed with which rich Celts could make these tools helped to make them powerful. They could easily clear new land, plough fields, and build homes. Then they could defend them.

◀ *This bucket, which was found at Aylesford in Kent, is made from wide wooden staves and bronze strips decorated with a swirly pattern. It was made in the first century BC by the Belgiae, a Celtic tribe who had newly arrived in Britain.*

The Celts were also skilled at rearing horses; they used horses in war, in hunting, in farming and for transport. They made horse-drawn carts and chariots. Unlike most of their enemies, they rode horses in battle.

The Celts' love of horses was expressed through their crafts and beautiful art. For their chariots, and for the horses' harnesses, their smiths made intricate metal fittings. Horses appear on many of their coins.

▲ An enamelled bronze plaque, probably part of a harness. It shows the Celts' skill at working with metal, and their love of horses which they adorned with beautiful trappings.

◄ This Celtic coin was used in Britain in the first century AD. The Celts often depicted horses on their coins.

A Roman writing in the third century AD, commented on the Celts' skill with enamel: 'They say that the barbarians who live in the Ocean pour these colours on to heated bronze and they stick fast, and grow as hard as stone, with the designs made in them.' The craftsmen laid powdered glass on a part of the metal, then heated it in an oven until it melted and stuck fast.

11

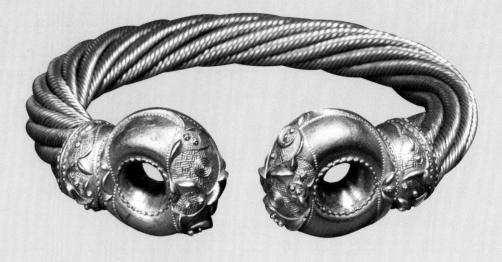

▶ A beautiful gold torque (neckband) made of threads of gold twisted like a rope. The torque was found at Snettisham, in Norfolk, part of the territory of the Iceni people. It could, perhaps, have belonged to Boudica, Queen of the Iceni.

Celtic artists

The Celts' artistic skills were used on everyday objects and jewellery: swords, scabbards, shields, harnesses, mirrors, neckbands (called 'torques') and coins. The richest and most beautiful would be for the wealthy chiefs and their families.

Celtic craftsmen must have been kept busy. Some of the hoards found have been scrap. These were metal pieces, chopped up and crumpled, ready to be melted down and made into something new.

▶ A decorated bronze cover for a shield. The cover was found in the River Thames, at Battersea in London. Can you spot a Celtic 'face' looking out at you?

One of these scrap hoards was found at Snettisham, in Norfolk, in 1994. It was a hoard of gold and silver scrap, including 175 torques. One gold torque was trapped and out of shape. When it was released it sprang straight back into shape – after 2,000 years!

◄ *This beautiful enamelled bronze brooch, shaped like a dragon, was probably made in England, in the first century AD.*

▼ *A bronze horseface, part of a harness made in the first century AD. It was found at Stanwick, in Yorkshire.*

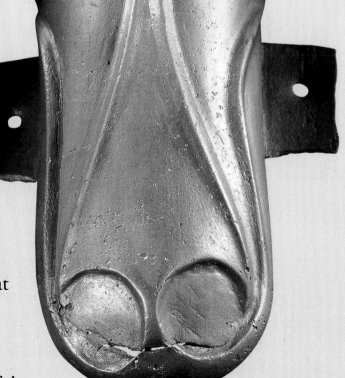

Celtic artists in Britain and Ireland used fascinating artistic tricks. One was to work faces into their designs. Sometimes the faces are hidden; then suddenly you see an owl or a cat or a horse peering out, or a secret 'eye' staring at you. But often they look at you openly. Another invention of Celtic artists was to use compasses to create designs. They did this on swords and mirrors especially. The results are beautiful.

chapter four

WHAT DID THE CELTS LOOK LIKE?

Some clues about what the Celts looked like come from the things they made. On coins, bucket and flagon handles, masks and sculptures we can see men with moustaches and swept-back hair.

Celts were probably clean; at least they used soap! 'Sopa' (soap) was a Celtic word which the Romans borrowed, and was probably a Celtic invention.

Romans and Greeks wrote about the appearance of the Celts. One Greek writer describes a strange hair style. He says the men had naturally blond hair, and they made it even paler by washing it with limewash. This treatment made it stick out in spikes. Some Celtic coins show this clearly. One story mentions hair so spiky 'it would pierce a falling apple'.

▲ A stone head, showing a man with curled-up moustaches and bulging eyes. The stiff, swept-back hair was a typical Celtic hairstyle.

A Roman writer describes a famous Celtic queen, Boudica, who led a rebellion against the Romans in 41 AD. 'Queen Boudica was huge and terrifying to look at, and she had a harsh voice. A great mass of red hair fell to her knees.' Another writer describes the Celt warriors fighting 'naked except for their weapons', and making a terrible din with 'countless horns and war trumpets,...and war cries'.

Celtic clothing

Celtic clothing was often rich and colourful. Many stories have long descriptions of what men and women looked like and how they dressed.

In one Welsh story, 'The Dream of the Emperor Maxen', a Roman leader sees men and boys who wear headbands, torques, armbands, belts and shoestraps, all of gold. A young woman with them 'wore white silk with gold brooches, a gold brocade coat and cloak fastened by a gem-encrusted brooch. Her hair stayed in place under a band of gold studded with rubies and she wore a wide belt of gold.' These were the richest Celts, dressed in their finest garments.

Although all but a few scraps of Celtic clothes have rotted away, many of their beautiful jewels and brooches survive for us to see.

◄ *Rich Celtic women often wore long jewelled brooches to pin their clothes. This brooch, decorated with animals, is from Tara, in Ireland.*

▼ *On the bronze back of this mirror are beautiful curving patterns, which were made using compasses – a Celtic design invention. Mirrors like this were made in England around the first century BC.*

There are many clues that Celts took great care over their appearance. One Roman poet teased his woman friend that she 'painted herself like a Celt'. Celt razors and tweezers were common, and mirrors were very valuable and often beautifully made. Obviously, the Celts used many of the same objects to improve their appearance as we do today.

A Greek writer of the first century BC, says: 'Physically the Gauls (the Roman word for Celts) are terrifying to look at, with deep rough voices. Their women are as tall as their husbands and just as strong.' He also says, 'The Gauls are tall, with moist white flesh.' And another Roman writer, Virgil, refers to their 'milkwhite necks' and the 'gold collars round them.'

chapter five

HOW WAS CELTIC LIFE
ORGANIZED?

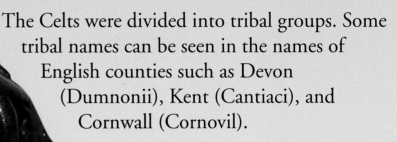

▼ *Celtic ploughs were sometimes pulled by oxen, as in this little sculpture of a man ploughing. On difficult soil, Celt farmers used hand ploughs to turn the earth.*

The Celts were divided into tribal groups. Some tribal names can be seen in the names of English counties such as Devon (Dumnonii), Kent (Cantiaci), and Cornwall (Cornovil).

The tribes were divided into smaller groups called clans. Apart from the chief and the chief's family, there were three other ranks or classes of people: the nobles, the free but not noble, and the unfree or slaves.

A number of women became famous as chiefs and warrior leaders. Boudica was the warrior queen of the Iceni tribe (see also page 14). After her defeat by the Romans and the death of 80,000 of her people, she poisoned herself. The Brigantians in the north of England had a woman chief, Cartimandua. Celtic kings and queens inherited their royal titles from their mothers, not from their fathers.

At the bottom of the clan were the unfree and slave Celts. They were labourers with no land and no rights. Above them were freemen who were mainly peasant farmers and less skilled craftsmen. They worked on the land and helped produce much of the clan's wealth. Freemen usually paid rent and a part of their produce to the chief. The chief did not grow crops; instead he owned cattle, and rented them out to the freemen.

Above the free men and women were the two groups of nobles. One group were warriors. These were the men who went off with their chief to raid other peoples when food or supplies were needed. They were his large personal fighting team, and they defended his fort.

In the other group of nobles were two kinds of people. One kind included the men and women of learning, such as judges, priests, astronomers, weather forecasters, mathematicians, doctors, keepers of the chief's family history and bards (poets). The other kind included all the master craftsmen, like blacksmiths, chariotmakers and metalworkers.

▲ *A famous modern statue of Queen Boudica, who led a rebellion against the Roman invaders (see panel on page 14). It stands beside the River Thames in London.*

Druids

People of learning were called druids. Although druids are sometimes called priests, they had many other duties. Druids were very important. They memorized the tribe's religion, law, history and poetry, keeping all the knowledge in their heads. The chief's own bard kept the family history. The bard also had to sing poems of praise to his chief, and attend battles – a bit like a sports reporter today!

The Celts had a written language, Ogham, but they did not use it for important or sacred knowledge. This was memorized and learned by heart. In Ireland a master poet called the ollamh 'had to memorize at least 350 stories, word for word'.

So Celtic knowledge was handed on orally from one generation to the next. This 'word of mouth' method was accurate, but from about the fourth or fifth century AD in Ireland, and later in Wales, some laws and history began to be written down.

One modern Irishwoman, Comte MacCarthy Reagh de Toulouse, can trace her ancestors back fifty-one generations, to AD 152. The family's history had been accurately remembered for centuries before it was written down.

In one part of Ireland the yearly rent for six of the chief's cows was 'a calf, a salted pig, three sacks of malt, half a sack of wheat, a handful of rush candles.' These details were part of the law; and they had to be remembered word for word.

Celtic customs and laws

The Romans and Anglo-Saxons did not come to Ireland and were rarely seen in mountainous and remote parts of Britain. So while the Celts in most of England were subdued, and in many ways became more Roman then English, the Celts living in Ireland and west Britain continued to be Celts.

These Celtic lands had schools and hospitals. One Irish law said that each territory had to have a hospital, with four doors, by a stream, which was free. The first Celt hospital in Ireland was founded in 397 BC.

In Ireland, criminals – even murderers – were not punished. Criminals had to compensate their victims properly; that was their punishment.

Feasts

Celtic chiefs gave regular feasts. These went on for days, with guests coming and going. Everyone sat on the floor in front of low tables, with the most important guest in the middle, next to the chief.

▲ This large, beautifully decorated cauldron was found at Gundestrop in Denmark. It had been placed in a marsh, possibly as an offering to a god.

There would be great vats of wine and mead (beer). Roast or boiled pork was a favourite food, with different portions given to different people: a leg for a king, a haunch for a queen, the head for the charioteer.

There was always entertainment provided by bards. Slaves served and fetched and carried. Slaves were common in British Celtic life. Many were sent to Rome and sold through slave markets. Payment was made in cattle – the price of a slave girl was three cows.

Trade

The slaves remind us that trade kept the Celtic world going. Celts fought and feasted, but their lives depended on trade. The chiefs' wine and tableware were imported. They and their wives liked luxuries and unusual novelties; in one Irish fort Barbary apes frolicked about.

Hengistbury, in Dorset, was one of the largest Celtic 'towns', and an industrial and trading centre. Metals were brought from west Britain to be melted down and turned into iron wares. There were probably wood and leather workshops, a mint for making coins, and a slave market.

The Celts could not have traded without roads. The remains of excellent Celtic roads have been found in parts of Britain.

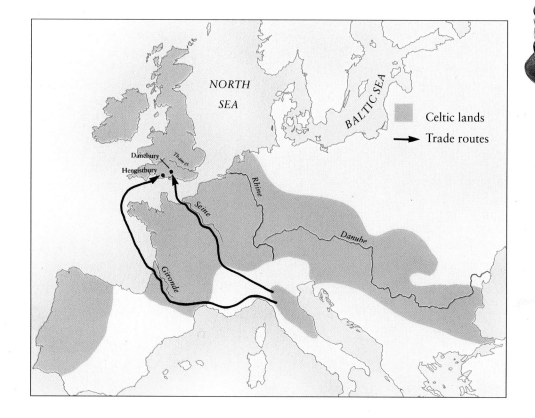

▲ A Celtic smith made this beautiful flagon. Notice the duck at the tip of the spout, and the handle in the form of a chained dog.

◀ A map showing the extent of Celtic lands in the last centuries BC and trade routes between Europe and English trading centres.

19

chapter six

WHAT RELIGION AND BELIEFS DID THE CELTS HAVE?

▼ *A part of the Gundestrop cauldron showing the Celtic horned hunting god Cerunnos, with some of his creatures. The god holds a torque in one hand and a snake with a ram's head in the other.*

For the Celts, gods and spirits were everywhere. Twisty trees, strangely shaped rocks, springs, dark pools and bogs hid mysterious powers. 'Britain is spellbound by magic,' said the Roman writer Pliny.

From Celtic tales we can understand what Pliny meant. In one, a sword speaks and recites its deeds. Another sword turns to strike its owner, who has done nothing that the sword can recite. A shield moans a warning of danger. A cup shatters after three lies are told over it.

Druids are often magicians in Celtic tales. They bring down snowstorms and raise fogs. They end droughts by shooting arrows in the air which fall and make springs. They hurl chunks of mountain through the air that flatten enemies.

Festivals and gods

Religious festivals were about harvest and sowing, crops and animals. At 'Samain' (1 November), when the Celtic year began, animals were slaughtered for the winter's food. 'Beltaine', on 1 May (May Day), was the next most important festival. Cattle were let out into the open fields. They were driven between two fires, to be protected by the firegod, Beli or Belenus.

Many Celtic gods were local, but a few were well-known. Lug was armed with a javelin and a sling, and was god of all the crafts. He was sometimes called 'Lug Longarm'. Epona was a goddess of horses and other wild creatures. She was also a goddess of fertility and plenty. In Ireland, Dagda, the 'good god', was tremendously strong. He carried a great club and a magic cauldron.

The Celts did not write down the names of their gods so we do not know who many of them were. But Roman writers mention them, and Roman inscriptions used the names of Celtic gods. For instance, the Roman town of Bath was called Aqua Sulis; Sulis was a local Celtic god of healing.

▲ *The head of a Roman-Celtic god from the north of England. It was found near Newcastle.*

◀ *This great white horse, carved on a chalk hill at Uffington in Oxfordshire, may be the Celtic goddess Epona.*

21

▲ *This huge figure carved in the chalk downs north of Cerne Abbas in Dorset, may be the Celtic god called Dagda in Ireland.*

▼ *This sculpture in Northumbria, shows the goddess Coventina as three water-nymphs. The Celts had a mystical belief in 'threes'; their gods often had three aspects, or faces.*

Sacred places

Celts had fears and superstitions as we do: 'The world isn't safe. Gods go round disguised as animals. Ogres come out of the sea. Always wear your torque to ward off evil.' How many of you like to wear a special bracelet or pendant for good luck?

The Celts wanted the gods on their side. They offered thanks to them and presented them with gifts. They often left gold and silver in lakes, for their gods to use.

Other favourite Celtic sacred places were fens, bogs, wells and groves of trees. Ireland still has springs and wells sacred to the Christian saint Brigid – named after the Celtic goddess Briggidda. Sacred groves could be scary to those who were not Celts. The Roman writer, Lucan, said about one grove that the wind never blew through the trees; birds were too frightened to perch on the branches.

A Roman writing about Celtic belief in life after death in the first century AD, says: 'They lend each other amounts of money which they agree can be paid back in the Other World; they are so convinced that souls are immortal.'

◀ *A Celtic 'cart-burial'. A Celtic chief would often be buried with a cart or chariot, or its frame and wheels. These chariot wheels have iron rims, a technique invented by the Celts.*

After death

The Celts believed that after death there was life in the 'Other World'. After a time the soul of the dead came back from the Other World, in another body.

Buried kings took large amounts of equipment to their graves, almost as if they were going on holiday. The Parisi chiefs in Yorkshire took a cart or chariot, as well as weapons and drinking horns; they were the only 'cart burials' in Britain. One king took a birchbark hat, fishhooks and toenail clippers.

Druids as priests

The Druids had duties as priests but they had other responsibilities as well. They were educated people who taught and travelled. They looked after the law and education, as well as religion.

The word druid comes from 'dru', meaning oak tree. Julius Caesar wrote about the Druids: 'They officiate at the worship of gods; they regulate public and private sacrifices, and give rulings on religious questions. Large numbers of young folk flock for instruction to them. They act as judges... Druid knowledge is oak knowledge, or great knowledge...' To become a druid took twenty years of study, mainly learning by heart!

chapter seven

WHAT STORIES DID THE CELTS TELL AND WHAT LANGUAGE DID THEY SPEAK?

▶ *This stone in County Kerry, Ireland, is inscribed with lines of different lengths, in a kind of Celtic writing called Ogham.*

Welsh and Irish stories were told at feasts, whenever they were requested by the chief . The bard sat close to the chief, and was served a tender portion of meat. Bards knew enormous numbers of stories, which they learnt by heart over many years. When asked to tell a story they had to be ready with the right one.

▶ *A page from the Book of Kells, produced by Irish monks in the eighth century. The monks have used many of the same designs as those produced by earlier Celtic craftsmen in bronze and iron.*

When the Welsh stories, called the Mabinogi, were written down, probably in the eleventh century AD, they contained the oldest Celtic Welsh tales. These are still told from memory, and new versions are written and published.

In Ireland Celtic stories were written down after the country became Christian. There was no Christian taboo against writing down important knowledge. Soon many were written down, then copied by monks. Many more were probably lost. Like the Welsh stories, the Irish tales are still told aloud from memory, and retold in books. They are like Westerns, full of cattle raids (rustling), murders, miraculous escapes, one-to-one combats (like shoot-outs) and revenge. One of the best is the tale of 'The Cattle Raid at Cooley'.

Magic and monsters

Celtic stories are full of magic. A druid hears an ant eighty km away. A boy hero stops 150 spears with a toy shield. A stone throne shrieks when the true king sits in it. Heads get cut off and then put on again back to front.

Body-changing was a favourite marvel. When two swineherd friends became enemies through magic, they changed to hawks and fought for two years, making a terrible din; they changed into otters and fought for a year, then stags, dragons, and lastly eels.

The Story of the Celtic language

The Celtic stories we know are only from Ireland, Wales, and the Western Isles and Highlands of Scotland. The Romans, and later the English, imposed their language on most of England and southern Scotland. The Celtic languages died, and in nearly all of England, except Cornwall, the Celtic stories died with them.

Except in west Cornwall, Celtic languages died out as speech. But Celtic words do survive in English, enough to remind the English of their Celt origins. These are some of the oldest words in English, words used for over two thousand years.

▲ A mountain valley in North Wales. When the Romans came, and after them the Anglo-Saxons, many British Celts fled into such remote areas of western Britain, taking their language and traditions with them.

Many names of large English rivers are Celtic. The Exe, Axe, Esk and Usk river names come from the Celtic word 'uisc' (in Gaelic 'uisge') meaning water. (The same word makes 'whisky', from 'usquebaugh', meaning water of life.) Thames, Tamar, Tavy and Taff come from a Celtic word meaning smooth or broad river.

Some mountain and hill names are Celtic . 'Moel', which is Welsh for a hill, gives us the Malvern Hills. Pennygant in Yorkshire is probably 'penn y gwynt', 'the height of the wind'.

Celtic words describe parts of the English landscape. In southern England a combe is a valley; it was borrowed from the Welsh, 'cwm', a hollow. And Irish and Scottish Celtic words in Gaelic have entered the English language: crag, cairn, glen, clan, claymore, ptarmigan, slogan. In other words, there are still Celtic words 'galore' (another Gaelic word) to be found in English.

▼ *The River Usk, in Wales. The word 'Usk' comes from the Celtic word 'uisc', meaning water.*

chapter eight

WHAT HAPPENED TO THE CELTS ?

After AD 43 England, Wales and southern Scotland became parts of a Roman province. For three hundred years, Britain slowly became more Roman and less Celtic.

But other British Celts kept their Celtic customs and speech, especially in mountainous Wales and northern England, and in Cornwall. They were able to keep their customs and their gods.

A few years after the Romans left, the Anglo-Saxons, later called the English, invaded Britain. They soon conquered nearly all of England, though they were kept out of Wales, Scotland and most of Cornwall.

Many British Celts fled to Wales and Cornwall. Cornish and Welsh people fled to Brittany in north-west France. The language which they took became Breton. Fifteen hundred years later speakers of Breton and Welsh can still talk to each other! About the same time, the Scoti tribe left Ireland and settled in Scotland, giving Scotland its name, and bringing the Irish Gaelic language to Scotland.

▼ *According to legend, these ruins on the cliffs at Tintagel in Cornwall may be the remains of the palace of Arthur, the Celtic king who defeated the English in battle about AD 500.*

As English rule spread, Celtic speech, place names, gods and stories, faded. But like the Romans, the English conquerors stayed away from Ireland. And people in out-of-the-way Cornwall, remote Scotland and mountainous Wales saw only an occasional English 'foreigner'.

English takes over

Over the centuries, the English went on invading Scotland, Ireland and Wales, taking their language with them. They passed laws making Welsh, Irish, or Scots Gaelic difficult or impossible to use. In the nineteenth century the Welsh language was banned in schools and law courts.

In the 1700s and early 1800s, thousands of crofters (small farmers) were driven from the Scottish Highlands. Many went to Nova Scotia (New Scotland), in Canada: 200,000 Gaelic speakers lived there in 1900. In 1865, Welsh speakers fled to Patagonia, in South America, where they set up a Welsh-speaking community.

▲ *Two centuries ago Scottish clansmen were still fighting each other just like their Celtic ancestors. They still 'fight' each other every year at the Highland Games.*

▼ *Ancient Celtic traditions live on at the annual Welsh eisteddfods – festivals of music, drama and poetry.*

The Celtic languages are alive now. They are spoken and taught in Wales, Scotland and Ireland. Wales has two official languages, Welsh and English, and two names, Cymru and Wales.

Celtic traditions survive too. Stories like the 'Cattle Raid of Cooley' are remembered and told. At ceilidhs in the Western Isles and in Ireland, people still enjoy singing, dancing and telling stories, just as the Celts always did.

GLOSSARY

Archaeologists People who study objects and remains from ancient times.

Barbarians Brutal or uncivilized people.

Barbary Ape A type of ape from northern Africa.

Bards Celtic poets and storytellers.

Bronze Metal, made from copper and tin.

Cauldron A large, heavy pot used for heating liquids.

Ceilidh The Gaelic word for a social gathering or party.

Chariot A two-wheeled vehicle used in war in ancient times.

Enamel Metal decorated with a colourful glassy substance.

Excavate To dig up.

Flagon A large vessel for holding drink.

Gaelic Any of the closely-related languages of the Celts in Ireland, Scotland and the Isle of Man.

Granaries Storehouses for grain.

Hamlets Very small villages.

Hebrides Islands off the west coast of Scotland.

Hoard A store of something, often hidden away.

Invade To enter a hostile country as an enemy.

Javelins Light spears which were thrown by hand.

Looms Frames for weaving thread.

Menaced Threatened.

Migrations Movements of people, from one place, or country, to another.

Mystical Having a sacred, or secret meaning.

Orally By word of mouth.

Rampart A defensive wall.

Refuge Shelter from attack.

Shrines Holy or sacred places.

Smith Another name for a blacksmith, someone skilled in working with metal.

Smithy A forge or workshop of a blacksmith.

Staves Wide strips of wood.

Superstitions Beliefs in magic.

Taboo Something which is forbidden or disapproved of.

Trappings Horse equipment such as reins, harness etc.

BOOKS TO READ

Atlas of Ancient Worlds by Dr Anne Millard (Dorling Kindersley, 1994)
Clues from the Past by Robin Place (Wayland, 1995)
History in Evidence by Barry M. Marsden (Wayland, 1989)
The Celts by Robin Place (Macdonald Educational, reprinted 1982)
What do we know about the Celts by Hazel Mary Martel (Heinemann, 1995)

PLACES TO VISIT

British Museum
Great Russell Street, London

The museum has examples of Celtic metalwork, jewellery, weapons, crafts etc. in the Pre-historic and Romano-British Department.

Gloucester City Museum
Brunswick Road, Gloucester.

The museum has an exhibition of Celtic metalwork including the famous Birdlip Mirror.

National Museum of Ireland
Kildare Street and 7-9 Merrion Row
Dublin.

The museum has an extensive collection of Celtic gold ornaments and early Christian metalwork.

Ulster Museum
Botanic Gardens, Belfast.

The museum houses collections of Irish archaeological material including from the time of the early Celtic invasions of Ireland.

There are many Celtic remains in the Hebrides, off the Scottish coast and on the Aran Isles, off the west coast of Ireland.

In England you can visit:

Butser Iron Age Village, Hampshire

Archaeologists have reconstructed a Celtic village where they try to live as the Celts did, growing the same type of crops and raising the same breeds of farm animals as those of the Celts.

Danebury Hill Fort.
Nr Winchester, Hampshire.

A visit to the excavated remains of this Celtic fort provides a very good idea of how the fort was constructed.

Maiden Castle
Near Dorchester, Dorset.

The remains of this large Iron-age Celtic fort are situated a few miles south of Dorchester, in Dorset.

INDEX

Numbers in **bold** refer to pictures

Anglo-Saxons 5, 28
Arthur, King **28**
artists 12, 13

bard 17, 18, 24
blacksmiths 11, 17
Book of Kells **25**
Boudica, Queen of the Iceni 14, 16, **17**
Brittany 28

'cart-burial' **23**
cauldron (see Gundestrop Cauldron)
ceilidhs 29
Celtic
  appearance 14, **14**, 15
  artistic skills 11, **11**, 12, **12**, 13, **13**, **15**, **19**
  clothing 9, 15
  crafts 10, 11, 12, 13
  customs 17, 18
  homeland 5
  laws 17, 18
  love of horses 10, 11, **11**
  migrations **6**
  names 16, 27
  religious beliefs 21–3
  words 7, 16, 27, **27**

Cerne Abbas chalk figure **22**
chiefs **4**, 5, 9, 16, 19, **23**, 24
coins 4, 11, **11**, 12
Cornwall 5, 9, 26, 28, **28**

Danebury hill fort 8, **8**
druids 17, 20, 23, 25

eisteddfod **29**

farmers 9, 11, 16, **16**
feasts 18, 19, 24
festivals 21
fields 9
forts 5, **5**, 7, **7**, 8, **8**, 9, **9**, 16

Gaelic (see languages)
gods 20, **20**, 21, **21**, 22, **22**
Gundestrop Cauldron **18**, **20**

Hengistbury 19
Highland games **29**
hill fort **5**, 8, **8**

Ireland 5, 6, 7, **7**, 9, **9**, 13, 18, 26

jewellery 5, 12, **12**, **13**, 15

languages
  Breton 28
  Celtic 5, **6**, 7, 8, 26–7, **26**, 28, 29
  English 26, 27, 29
  Gaelic **6**, 8, 27, 28, 29
  Ogham 17, **24**
  Welsh 27, 29
Maiden Castle **5**
metalworkers 10, 19

poetry 17

roads 8, 19
Romans 5, 14, 18, 21, 28

Scotland 5, **6**, 7, 26, 28, 29, **29**
shrines 8
slaves 19
stories 15, 17, 24-5, 26, 29

torque 12, **12**, 13
trade 5, 19, **19**
tribes 7, 16, 28

Wales 17, 26, **26**, 26-7, 28, **29**
warriors 14, 16

Picture acknowledgements
The publishers would like to thank the following for permitting the reproduction of their pictures: Lesley and Roy Adkins Picture Library 8; Ancient Art and Architecture Collection 9, 16, 17(top), 18, 26-7; copyright British Museum cover (right), 4(lower), 10, 12(top), 13(top), 23; C. M. Dixon cover (right),14, 15(top), 21(top), 22(both); Eye Ubiquitous/J. B. Pickering 26; ffotograff /C. Aithie 29; Robert Harding /M. Collier 5, /D. Lomax 6, 7, /Roy Rainford 28, /G. Roli 29(top); Tony Stone Worldwide /D. McNicol 21(lower); Werner Forman Archive 24, /British Museum 4(top), 11(lower), 12(lower), 13(lower), 15(lower), 19 /Musée Archeologique de Breteuil cover (main picture) and 11(top), /National Museum, Copenhagen title page and 20; Trinity College Library, Dublin 25. The maps on pages 6 and 19 are by Peter Bull Design.